WHEN YOU ARE FACING A DIVORCE

DIFFICULT TIMES SERIES

WHEN YOU ARE FACING A DIVORCE

JAN JOVAAG ANSORGE

Augsburg

MINNEAPOLIS

WHEN YOU ARE FACING A DIVORCE

Large-quantity purchases or custom editions of this book are available at a discount from the publisher. For more information, contact the sales department at Augsburg Fortress, Publishers, 1-800-328-4648, or write to: Sales Director, Augsburg Fortress, Publishers, P.O. Box 1209, Minneapolis, MN 55440-1209.

Cover Design by David Meyer
Book Design by Jessica A. Klein

ISBN 0-8066-4361-7

The paper used in this publication meets the minimum requirements of American National Standard for Information Sciences—Permanence of Paper for Printed Library Materials, ANSI Z329.48-1984. ♾ ™

Manufactured in the U.S.A.   AF 9-4361

06   05   04   03   02   2   3   4   5   6   7   8   9   10

❧ Contents ❧

❧ *Introduction* ❧

This book is intended for those who are facing divorce and yet care enough about their marriages, themselves, and their families to seek guidance from a variety of sources as they go through the process of divorce, and as they learn to live with this life-altering decision. Many times, we speak of divorce as an event occurring on a specific day. In this book, I am approaching divorce as a process that begins long before the legal day of divorce and ends much later.

I am writing as a survivor of divorce, a process that began in my life ten years ago. I am going to tell you my story from my point of view and hope that in its particularities it has some universality.

The night my husband told me that he was in another relationship, my response was to leap from my chair, start pacing, and repeat, "There is nothing left." The agony that began that moment was unrelieved for months and months.

The agony attacked on all fronts: physical, mental, emotional, and spiritual. Many times I simply could not function normally. The day following his revelation was the first day of the school year. I was to teach a new course I had designed over the summer. At the end of that first day, I had no idea what I had said to my classes, and for days and weeks I would hear myself talk in class and wonder what sense any of it made.

Three days after the revelation, I began keeping a journal, something I would recommend to everyone. It helped me sort my feelings and bring some order to chaotic thoughts and events. My first journal entry:

> *I Have Nothing Left*
> *Inside Myself*
> *Alone*
> *Aching*
> *Sick*
> *Too hurt to write*
> *Pain*
> *Nausea*
> *Fear*
> *Lost*
> *Alone, alone, Lonely*
> *Tired*
> *Weary*
> *Death of Hope*
> *Birth of Despair*

All those feelings were my companions for too long. It has been a difficult journey back to a meaningful and hopeful life since that dreadful revelation. But I am glad I have made it this far.

From time to time throughout this book, I ask questions. I hope you will take the time to thoughtfully respond to those questions, preferably in your personal journal, but otherwise in conversations with your spouse, your friends, or in the form of interior monologues.

❧ *Chapter One* ❧

Is Divorce the Right Solution?

When we are faced with the prospect of divorce, we need to examine our marriage with regard to the past, our present situation, and the future, in the ramifications of our decisions for ourselves and our families. Nothing in this process is easy and the solution to our difficulties is rarely absolutely clear. Anguish in its many forms—sadness, pain, anger, loneliness, uncertainty—are guaranteed to be present as we work our way through the difficult times ahead. But before we get there, let's begin at the beginning. . . .

The July afternoon is sunny, warm, and breezy. The wind picks up and the bride's veil scoots off her head as she starts down the aisle in the garden church. The violins play on; the congregation smiles; the bride laughs, dives for her veil, and reattaches it; the groom waits with tender love in his heart for this carefree spirit who is coming toward him, this barefoot bride with yards and yards of tulle wafting behind her.

Afterward, the wedding party and all the guests gather to eat, to dance, and to toast this lovely couple on their festive day. The groom's mother's toast is her wish list for the couple.

$\mathcal{A}$ Mother's Wishes
for Her Son and His Bride

My dear children, I want you to be virtuous in your marriage—to be loyal, trustworthy, honorable, respectful, faithful—I want you to be good to one another and to be good for one another. Consider your thoughts, words, and actions. Are they constructive or destructive for your mate, for your marriage? Dear children, live life lovingly.

I want you to love each other so much that each of you can fully relax and bask in that love—even take it for granted!

I want each of you to think, now and always, that you are the lucky one in this marriage—you are the one who got the prize!

I want you to know that I—along with this host of witnesses—embrace you and surround you with love on this holy day and throughout the days of your lives together. Seek us whenever you need us or want us.

I want you to keep God as the centerpiece of your life together. Be faithful to God and each other; love—and be loved by—God and each other and those whose lives touch yours; and keep your hope in God, in life, and in your marriage.

And be thankful—for your love, for your marriage, for one another, for your friends and families, for good and abundant food, for health, for work and play, for your talents, for strength to survive hardships; be thankful for each day, for each season, for each year that you share throughout your lives.

May you, my dear children, abide in the peace that passes all understanding and in the joy that wells up deep within and fills our cups to overflowing.

BEFORE THE DIVORCE

Amazing. Isn't this how many of us began? Didn't we want these same wishes for ourselves? In fact, weren't these wishes actually the expectations we had for our marriages? What has caused us to find ourselves in such a far place from those pure and heartfelt desires? Did we stop being virtuous? When and why did loyalty, trust, respect, and faithfulness begin deteriorating? Did the erosion begin with an event, words, infidelity, physical or verbal abuse, an addiction, selfishness, carelessness? Do you long to go back to a certain point in your marriage and begin again from there?

Shortly after my divorce, I moved to a house on the same river where our married life had begun. One day I went for a boat ride past that first treasured home of ours. I remembered our Saturday morning breakfasts on the raft; parties with good friends when we tubed down the river, then barbecued steaks; I recalled taking long Sunday afternoon canoe trips on the lazy river and exploring the nearby Texas Hill Country on our motorcycles. My husband and I had great jobs, a wonderful place to live, boundless energy, and a world to discover. Life seemed to have rolled out its magic carpet, and I anticipated with delicious excitement the unfolding of the future. I could hardly believe I was so lucky! Indeed, as I slowly motored by that house of memories so many years and events later, I longed to go back to those days and begin again.

The first important step when contemplating divorce is to look back on the good years and ask: Is the damage that the marriage has since sustained irreparable? Can we pick up the fragments of the relationship and build anew? Or is the damage so severe that the broken marriage cannot be restored?

CONTEMPLATING DIVORCE

What do we need to do as we contemplate a divorce? Surely none of us decides to divorce without a great deal of agony. And usually we are so off-balance during this dramatic time that we are not even sure we can trust ourselves to make the right decision. Hopefully, we seek the aid of several guides to help us through this difficult process, but even as we seek their wisdom, we must remember that they are not the ones to live with the consequences of our decisions. We have to do that.

Counselors are one valuable guide for both parties in the divorce. Excellent and wise counselors can help us define our issues and help us see alternatives as well as teach us about patterns of behavior and communication problems. And we can feel free to talk openly with them; in fact, that is what we go there to do.

Suggestions:

- Shop for the right counselor for you. Does the counselor share your values? Does the counselor seem fair-minded? Wise? Will you learn something helpful from this person?

- Insist that your spouse go to counseling, too. A divorced friend once said that if he could do anything over, he would have insisted on going to counseling with his wife. He thought she was dealing with her own issues; he didn't realize his marriage was at stake.

- Sharing a counselor seems to be most helpful. Often a counselor will see a couple together and then meet with each person individually. The counselor then knows more about the situation.

Other helpful sources we can look to as we struggle with this life-altering decision are trusted and wise friends and family members, recommended books about divorce and recovery, and visits with honest people who have divorced, as well as those who remained married even though they had to deal with serious, divisive issues.

I had three particularly important personal guides during this period. One of these was my father, a ninety-year-old retired pastor who, despite his strong convictions about marriage and divorce, wanted me to leave the marriage. He said, "Close that chapter of your life, and get on with your wonderful future." The second guides were my three children, who ranged in age from twenty-three to sixteen. I listened to them, talked to them, and thought about them throughout the process. I also realized that they were confused, as I was, and that nothing they said would necessarily be the same five or ten years later. They, too, were caught in the middle of the drama and could not predict the variety of outcomes any more than I could. But their voices and hearts were very important to me. My third guide was Jesus, who said we should forgive "seventy times seven," but he also threw the money changers out of the temple. I regarded marriage as holy, and I felt it had been and was being desecrated. I remained uncertain about my decision for a long time.

This time of uncertainty is very difficult; we do not know what we want to happen or what will happen regardless of our wishes. Our spouse may want a divorce when we are not ready for that step, or they may be uncertain about what they want, and their uncertainty contributes to ours; in fact, it may cause ours. Indeed, their uncertainty may be the controlling factor.

What can I do? What should I do? Wait, pray, seek peace and understanding and compassion. I want the peace that passes all understanding. I want to live life lovingly. I pray that the best course for this opens before me before too long. This uncertainty—his and thus mine—is dreadful.

Daily Life as We Contemplate Divorce

While we live in the turmoil of uncertainty, we must continue our daily lives. We go to work, we continue to be parents, we have household responsibilities. All these tasks seem hopelessly difficult. How can we possibly function at all normally as we struggle with our failing marriages?

The pain in my stomach does not stop. I am not function-ing. My classes, my children, and I all suffer. I hardly sleep; I jerk awake again and again. My whole body lurches. Is there peace anywhere?

Doing the laundry, buying groceries, putting together a meal all seemed beyond me. I remember facing a sink full of dishes and feeling overwhelmed. One day as I sorted the laundry and put in a load, I just wept. Would I not be doing this small, intimate task for long? Another time I went into the grocery store, the same one I had shopped in for years, yet everything seemed unfamiliar. How could I choose what food to buy? How could I bear to see other people going through the normal motions of grocery shopping? I started down the aisles, but I chose noth-ing. I left the empty basket and the store.

Suggestions:

- Send your spouse to the grocery store.
- Enlist help from your friends if you need it.
- Discover what helps you regain balance. One friend found that focusing on her graduate work helped her deal with the turmoil in her life. Another friend cleaned her house thor-oughly, claiming that activity was beneficial to her well-being. Another played hand after hand of solitaire to restore a sense of order to his life. Another friend jogged three miles a day.

SUFFERING AS WE
HEAD TOWARD DIVORCE

During this time we suffer in so many ways. We feel sad, angry, worthless, unwanted, unlovable, lonely. The anguish is nearly unendurable as the marriage falters and fails. Pain never ceases, day or night. We may long for the time just before everything fell apart. The ease of that life is now gone and in its place is this dreadful suffering.

Gloomy days, gloomy nights. I ache. I long for calmness in my soul. I pray for calmness, for strength, for this ugliness to be lifted from my shoulders, my worn, burdened shoulders. I need a balm in Gilead to heal my wounded, broken heart.

I want my life to be over or new—I cannot bear this torture chamber much longer. I am sick with grief, loss, death. I am emptied of joy or spirit. Oh God, help me bear it all! I am too sad for too many days, hours, minutes—it's all agony. I dread each day, each hour.

The utter sadness of it all overwhelms me. The hopes and dreams have gone so far away. Our whole history seems to be set in a gray cast. Oh, my husband, where was your judgment? My heart aches for you, for our children, for us. Can we ever hope to smile in joy again? Or will our lives always be touched with sadness? Sorrow is my cloak now.

ANGER AS WE FACE DIVORCE

Pain and sorrow are not our only reactions. We also experience anger, and that anger may turn into a rage greater than we had ever before experienced.

One day my son came home unexpectedly and found me reading a book about anger. He said, "Mom, why are you reading that book? You're never angry." We hadn't yet told the children about our situation, so he didn't know about the dreadful rage within me that I was trying to learn more about.

Many of us are taught or learn along the way that anger is bad, destructive, and an out-of-control emotion, so we tend to bury it or work it out doing some physical work, or count to ten and then say nothing. We don't want that emotion to surface. We fear it may destroy something that we do not want destroyed.

On the other hand, we may use anger to cover other emotions that we are even more afraid to face. Perhaps without it we would be depressed, or feel guilty, sad, lonely, forsaken, or threatened, so we put on this armor of anger to protect ourselves.

It is important to face our anger to see if it is the true emotion we are experiencing and also to realize its constructive and destructive uses in our lives as we go through divorce. Anger can give us the energy we need to go on. It can bring us relief from depression and provide the impetus we need for productive activity. It also can release us to speak about issues that need to be out in the open—issues that have been sensed or dreaded but never discussed. However, anger can also be destructive: in its grips we can blurt out damaging insults or accusations we don't really mean but can never retract. Even worse, if unleashed and uncontrolled, anger may lead to acts of violence and cruelty.

I wrote about my anger into my journal frequently. When I was venting my deepest anger, my handwriting would be violently out of control, but that violence didn't harm anyone.

I rage. I rage. He has to get out of my life. He is only pain. I cannot bear the torment. I hate this life. The poison is everywhere. It permeates everything.

Anger often comes because we feel we are powerless and impotent. Our present, our future, even our pasts seem completely out of our control. How could someone else determine so much of our lives without consulting us? It seems utterly unfair. Choices have been made that affect our lives so deeply and permanently, yet we are not told about those decisions, much less asked to participate in the decision making.

A deep anger brews within. How could he make choices that completely alter my life, indeed the children's lives, without asking me? And he continues to make decisions that lead to more distance and distrust between us. I feel myself withdraw. I quit. I quit. I cannot bear this rage borne out of my impotence.

🪶

My anger overpowers me. I realize with such certainty and clarity what a dreadful predicament I am in. I have a broken family with no base and a shattered marriage, and I am powerless to alter one iota of this mess.

Questions to consider:

- Have you discovered the real reasons for your anger?

- Are you dealing with that anger constructively? Elaborate.

❧ Chapter Two ❧

Losses We Must Face

So much of life involves loss, but the breakdown of a marriage involves dramatic, sudden, life-altering, often shattering losses. We lose our innocence, our trust, our hopes for the future, our mate, the wholeness of a family, our daily routines, our role in the community, our identities, and we often lose our self-esteem. The losses we suffer affect many others as well—our families, our friends, and our communities.

LOSS OF TRUST

The word *trust* becomes a very big word when we face divorce. When we first learn about our spouse's behavior that is hurting us so deeply, we begin to distrust. But as time goes on and there are more revelations and more broken promises and more lies covering other behaviors, our trust breaks down further. Then we may feel like we will never know the truth, and that we won't be able to count on truth ever again. Finally, truth and falsehoods become so difficult to untangle that we begin to wonder how much of our shared history was fiction.

In my situation, once one lie began, it spawned others, until my ex was seemingly caught in a spider web—a web of lies, half-truths, and concealed truth; then to remember what was a lie and what was truth became hopelessly difficult for him. As I lost my trust in his veracity both in words and actions, I also lost my trust in his judgment and his opinions. So much of what he said and did was designed to defend or hide his behavior. His words and actions no longer reflected the beliefs and the values I thought we shared. As a result of this breakdown of trust, I could no longer reveal to him my feelings, my thoughts, my private self; I had learned that he could hurt me too profoundly.

Questions to consider:

- Can you again trust someone who has shown no regard for your intimate feelings? How would you go about restoring that trust?

- Can you again trust someone who has lied to, cheated, or betrayed you?

- Can trust be reestablished with someone who has chosen behavior that destroys your family?

- Are you remaining trustworthy throughout this difficult time?

- What does the word *trust* mean to you?

Loss of Meaning

Home and the family are of utmost importance to many of us whose marriages are failing. Indeed, much of our anger and our sadness stems from the realization that our hopes and dreams for our marriages and our families are destroyed. We invested so much of ourselves, so much work, thought, energy, and time into something that has been thoughtlessly discarded or damaged by our mates, and now all that

work and all those dreams seem so meaningless and
we are filled with an emptiness.

*My life has been a futile struggle. I have ended with noth-
ing. The children inherit chaos and confusion, not the
solid loving home they thought they had.*

🍃

*Futility! That is the feeling I have about my life in this
marriage. It has all been for naught. Is it also futile to
continue? Is my whole life going to be used trying to get
past this, trying to put something meaningful into our
relationship, and then perhaps discover that the effort has
been for naught? I don't know. I don't know that I want to
try anymore. Life looks so dismal, so confining, so meager,
so self-centered. Is this all there is? What is the value of
my life? I feel like I'm not doing anybody any good anymore. I am lost and floundering and want to break free,
but I don't know how; I don't know if it is possible. The
past is me now. I am changed, utterly changed, by it. My
present self is a coming together of my whole history, and
I wish so that my history were different. This is not the
history I chose; this is not the life I wanted, hoped for, and
worked for. But it is my life. Where do I go from here?
What do I do? How can I reassemble a life that has a purpose, some meaning, and some hope? I do not know.
Robert Frost's words come to me frequently: I have "nothing to look backward to with pride, and nothing to look
forward to with hope." This is death in life—and I really
hoped to avoid such a life-shattering experience.*

🍃

I have failed. This marriage has failed. My goal in life is gone. I have no hope. I give up. Jesus, help me get through my coming days. Amen

Questions to consider:

- What goals and dreams in your life are affected by this marital breakdown?
- What of value can you recover from this experience?

Loss of Control over Our Own Lives

Sometimes, whatever is driving the marriage to ruin—whether it is addiction, infidelity, some form of abuse, or another problem—seems to have more control of us than we have of our own lives. We can feel helpless as these behaviors rage on. The refusal to change these destructive behaviors often leads to divorce because we need to regain control over our own lives.

Liz dreaded opening the door to their apartment night after night. Her husband would be on the other side of that door. Would he be drunk? Violent? Ready to pass out? Or, blessed thought, would he be sober? The anxiety that came from not knowing became intolerable; she developed health problems and finally knew she had to end the marriage.

Questions to consider:

- Have you lost control of your life? What specific behaviors (whether actions, words, or non-verbal messages) contribute to that loss?
- How can you regain control of your life?

Loss of Identity

Another difficulty we have to face when we divorce is that we lose our identity and are given a new identity, one that for many of us is shameful: *I am divorced.* Surely not me! It is not easy to fill out even the most impersonal forms that call for our marital status: married, single, widowed, *divorced*. It is even more difficult to acknowledge and actually give voice to that new identity at work, at church, to people we meet socially. And, by being addressed as Ms., women bear additional constant exposure to their divorced status. Luckily for men, they remain Mr., no matter their marital state.

In addition, we are used to living in the comfortable position that marriage itself bestows upon us. Social acceptance and a sense of belonging are ours just because we are married. And until we are once again single, we don't know what that will be like. Will we feel left out or awkward when we go places alone? Will people feel uncomfortable with us as single people? Will we be perceived as one of society's failures?

Finally, we are identified as part of a couple, as "so-and-so's" wife or husband; then we are put into a certain slot. For example, we discover that the man who fixes furnaces is married to an esteemed artist. Click, click, click go our minds, and we now have a revised version of the man who fixes furnaces. This reevaluation is not necessarily good, but it often happens. When we are married, we are not only seen for who we are individually; we are also partially identified with our mates. In marriage, we become one on many levels.

These profound changes in identity are unavoidable. However, the loss of married identity does not plunge you into a permanent void. You do gain a new identity, one which is perhaps more true to who you are. In time, this new identity will become comfortable and even rewarding.

Questions and ideas to consider:

- If you changed your name when you were married, have you thought about changing your name when you divorce? A friend changed her last name to her mother's maiden name. Another woman changed her first and last names. Some women are reluctant to change their last names because it is the name they share with their children.

- Begin going places alone, if you don't do that already. Go to a movie, a coffeehouse, or for a walk. Take a trip. Stay in a hotel.

Loss of Self-Esteem

Losing our identity is only one way our self-esteem suffers. Much more devastating to us is that we feel unwanted, unlovable, and lonely. We doubt that our mate was ever glad or felt lucky to be married to us. We feel worth less, yes, worthless.

I feel like I am the drudge, the work-a-day world. I'm back to reality and dreariness—I hold no adventure, no wonder,

just dull sameness and routine. I am a symbol of responsi-
bilities that saddle him and keep him from living life fully,
from what he calls "following his bliss," and "letting the
flood of life flow freely."

LOSS OF A MATE

In spite of feeling unwanted and unloved, even
abused, we still miss our mates when they are gone. We
miss small things like the daily routines we shared with
our spouse (I missed waking up to the smell of the
morning coffee!), we miss someone to share household and financial responsibilities, we miss someone
to talk to about the children. Who else is so interested
in the little accomplishments and disappointments in
our children's lives? We miss the laughs, the private
humor, the person who shared so much history with
us. We sometimes lose the person we had thought was
our best friend, even our soulmate. But sometimes,
because of destructive behaviors, we must relinquish
parts of our lives that we will miss.

Questions to consider:

- What will you miss when you lose your spouse?
- What are some possible opportunities that will
  come from autonomy?

RAMIFICATIONS AND LOSSES FOR OTHERS

The losses are not ours alone. The family is ripped
apart; if children are involved, their love and trust for
their parents is shaken, because their parents are no

longer a unit. Instead they have to adjust to a new and different relationship with each parent. Their new reality is worlds away from what they had thought was their reality. Their lives are turned upside down. And children react to this stunning blow. Some children bitterly resent the parent whom they perceive to be the villain. Some play one parent against the other. Some children refuse to communicate about their losses, their anger, their feelings of abandonment. Some become rebellious or troubled; their grades fall, they choose bad friends, or they become isolated. Some get sick or hurt, trying to get their parents back together.

When ten-year-old Mike learned from his father that he was going to move out of the house and that he and Mike's mom were going to get a divorce, Mike wrote "I hate my dad" over and over again, more than one hundred times. His anger was inconsolable.

Questions to consider:

- How do we regain the trust of our children?

- How can we restore a sense of order and balance to this world of chaos in which they have suddenly been immersed?

- What losses do we as parental partners face? How can we continue to partner in this area of life when we divorce?

- Is the choice for divorce or for continuing the behavior that is leading to the divorce worth the pain we are causing the dear children entrusted to our care?

- Is it possible that in our situation the choice for divorce is the better choice for the children?

One morning shortly before Christmas, I was explaining to the children that we would be going to Florida for Christmas without their dad. I had carefully approached the subject and discussed it without realizing that my youngest son wasn't listening. He was absorbed in his latest issue of *Sports Illustrated*. When he finally looked up and said, "What?" I very briefly told him my last sentence: "Dad won't be going with us to Florida." He put his head down on the table and quietly wept. And he couldn't stop. I called my husband at his office and asked him to please come home. When he got there and joined me in trying to console our son, I asked, "Is she worth this?" "No," he answered. He went with us to Florida. But the truce, if it was that, didn't last.

Children of various ages experience divorce differently, and the needs, fears, and changes each child will encounter because of the divorce must be recognized and addressed. Most children trust that their family will always be together. When they discover that one parent is leaving, they are thrown into unfamiliar routines. Often they must move to a new place to live and divide their lives between two residences. Perhaps the most devastating loss, however, is the loss of innocence, a treasured and so important state and stage in our children's lives.

Resources to consult:

- *Healthy Divorce* by Craig Everett and Sandra Volgy Everett
- *Help: A Girl's Guide to Divorce and Stepfamilies* by Nancy Holyoke
- *When Children Grieve* by John W. James and Russell Friedman with Dr. Leslie Landon Matthews
- *Divorce Book for Parents* by Vicki Lansky
- *How to Talk to your Kids about Really Important Things* by Charles E. Schaefer and Theresa DiGeronimo

Our extended families also suffer. They ache for us and need to readjust their hopes and expectations as well. Family outings will forever be different. Weddings, funerals, graduations—all ceremonies, all celebrations, all holidays, are affected by a divorce.

And our friendships often suffer from our divorces. Friends can no longer invite both ex-spouses to the same gatherings. Often both parties are left off the guest list; it seems too awkward or rude to invite just one. Or the evening is for couples, or one remarries and old friends don't like the new spouse. And sometimes friends become wary—for one thing, if our marriages have failed, why not theirs?

❧ Chapter Three ✍

The Decision to Divorce

Throughout the divorce process, we become wounded. The separation of two people who were united as one cannot occur without emotional, psychological, physical, social, and spiritual wounding. The real decision that lies before us as we face divorce is which option holds more healing potential for us, for our families, for our communities, and, yes, even for our spouses. This is not easy to discern when we are in the middle of the chaos and feeling such excruciating pain that we are certain we have to flee from it or we will never recover. It is not easy even years later to determine which option would have been the best for all concerned.

No problems in life resolve quickly. Television misleads us all. Actions have far-reaching and long-lasting consequences. And we can't know the impact our choices will have—not entirely. I so often think of my decision to divorce and the consequences of that choice for the children. At the time, they seemed to think that the consequences of my not divorcing would be more damaging to them. I wonder if they still feel that way, or if they will ten or twenty or forty years from now. I hope my decision and my life will be the most positive possible, given the situation. That is all I can hope for.

We take the road that we take, and we cannot know how other choices would have turned out. If we choose divorce we may (though it is a futile task) ask ourselves if we could ever have regained trust and respect for our spouses. Would power and control issues have changed? Would the destructive behaviors have stopped? Could we have continued to love someone who has caused us so much pain? Could we have been forgiving, truly forgiving? Would the same wars have been continually replayed? Could we have experienced hope and joy and real intimacy? Could we have grown into the people we have become had we chosen differently?

OUR ROLE IN THE BREAKDOWN

Sometimes we feel responsible for the breakdown of the marriage and rehearse other scenarios for our marriages. We think "if only" I had done this or not done that, been this way or that way, then perhaps our marriages wouldn't be failing. But we cannot know what would have happened, "if only." Perhaps our marriages would have failed sooner. Perhaps not, but, regardless, dwelling on the "if onlys" is a fruitless use of time. We cannot alter the past one iota. And I think most of us can be confident that we invested our whole selves in the marriage—if we hadn't, we wouldn't suffer so much when it fails.

It's midnight. I lie in bed and think, and I weep. How could I—with the best of intentions, the highest hopes, the loftiest dreams, the deepest desires, and a heart filled with love—have failed so utterly?

Questions to consider:

- Are your friends who are in secure marriages any better than you?
- What have you learned about yourself that will be helpful in a future relationship?

Reading the Signs

Questions to consider:

- As we look for signs that might help us move toward a decision, are we seeing those signs and paying attention to them?
- Can we trust the signs that we think we see?
- Are we interpreting them correctly?

Early in our breakup, a counselor told me that frequently the one who initially wants to get out of the marriage ultimately wants reconciliation, and the one who initially wants to save the marriage files for divorce. After nine months of hoping for reconciliation, a sign led me away from seeking reconciliation and toward filing for divorce.

Together with our counselors, my husband and I decided we needed a break from the intense struggle we were experiencing and that a trial separation could help us decide what we should do. With the help of our counselors, we worked out the ground rules. His classes were over; mine were not, so he went to a friend's unoccupied country house fifty miles from home for what was to be a month. We were to talk once a week on the phone, and he could pick up his mail at the house once a week, but we wouldn't talk then. When he left, I armed him with a Bible, three books I had found helpful, and a journal.

The first Wednesday he was to call at ten o'clock at night. He forgot! I thought I would go crazy. I had been so anxious about that call, I had thought of little else for two days. An hour later, I called him. He told me he wouldn't apologize for forgetting and he wouldn't console me or tell me he loved me because "this was not the right time. These calls were supposed to be superficial visits." I was devastated. He admitted he had read nothing and written nothing. What, I wondered, was going on? He sounded so cold, so aloof, so distant.

Ten days later, I discovered the reason for that upsetting phone conversation and I also got the sign I needed—not the one I had wanted, but a definite sign.

When my husband came to pick up his mail, my son went out to give it to him; I watched from inside. My husband decided to check on the horses in the front pasture, so he took off his clean shirt and put it in his truck. From inside, I saw the glint of a necklace, something he had never worn before. I shot out the door and confronted him about the necklace. He said, "This old thing?" We walked together into the field. When we were out of earshot of our son, I looked carefully at the necklace, a silver hand holding a heart, yanked it off his neck, and told him "she" must have been at the ranch. He admitted that she had been. Yes,

they had had sex, "but not much," he added. As
though that made it okay! As we walked back to the
house, I slipped the necklace into the trash and then,
very quietly, told him that this was the sign I needed,
not the one I had hoped for, but now I knew it was
over. He told me not to be hysterical. I wasn't. I felt
calmer than I had felt in months. I excused myself and
went to be with our son, who was lying on our bed,
grieving. He knew what had happened. I lay down
beside him, put my arm around him, and told him it
was over. I promised him that we would have a good
life. I heard the truck start up, and realized David had
stayed long enough to dig in the trash and retrieve the
necklace I had slipped in there. I didn't mind. The
next day I began shopping for a lawyer.

*I am relieved. I no longer have to sort out truth from lies.
I got the clear sign I needed. Thank you, God. So much of
my anxiety through the years has been lifted from me and
the torment is past and I am glad.*

Of course, the certainty of what I should do and
the accompanying relief were not as constant as I had
hoped they would be. And I cannot imagine that anyone goes through divorce without misgivings.

Two months later, my husband decided he
wanted reconciliation. We continued to go to counseling, but there were no clear indications that reconciliation was the best course. The other woman
remained in the picture and in his life, and he made
no sacrifices or real attempts to change the destructive

behaviors; he remained unrepentant. No, I suspected that the wish for reconciliation was self-serving—an attempt to secure his place, his job, his reputation, his financial security.

Suggestions and questions:

- Define the issue that is driving you toward divorce. What is being done about that issue? Is the abuse continuing? Is the addict not seeking treatment? Is the infidelity a continuing problem?

- Will you ever be able to trust your mate again?

- Communicate with your spouse. I have heard that a couple's most significant communication takes place during a second date (do we want to continue this relationship?) and during the breakup of a marriage (do we want to continue this relationship?).

- Be as honest and straight with yourself, your spouse, and your counselor as possible. But don't resort to verbal cruelty, even if you want to.

- Don't hide from yourself or each other. This is no time for games or manipulation or ego retreats or aggressions.

- Take care of yourself through this highly stressful process. When we are suffering, we often don't take care of ourselves. Life seems to have little worth; but those feelings change in time and if we don't take care of ourselves, we will pay for it. So, eat nutritiously, get your rest, and exercise. No one is worth losing your health over.

THE LEGAL ASPECTS OF DIVORCE

The legal part of divorce is a more practical matter, but it, too, is complicated and difficult. When I recently looked through my divorce file, I was amazed at the bulk. I had forgotten how many letters floated between the lawyers articulating minor adjustments about the division of property, the responsibilities for the minor child, and the copies of the court orders and court dates that were set and reset.

Suggestions:

- Get the best lawyer. By that I mean someone trustworthy and loyal to you. And make sure your lawyer is assertive and smart. Interview more than one, and never share a lawyer with your spouse.

- Do not believe that your spouse will be on your side in a divorce. It is important to realize that the divorce settlement is a business transaction, not a way to regain your spouse's approval or love. Working out the settlement is, in fact, one of the first steps in your becoming independent.

The actual day of the divorce can be postponed again and again, and sometimes that waiting period, though tough, is important. Each time a new date is set, we must recommit ourselves to the divorce, and, in doing so, we also reconsider the possibility of reconciliation. That possibility may seem more and more remote, as it did for me, and then the decision to divorce seems increasingly right.

The day of my divorce, a hot May afternoon, I waited for my lawyer on the sunbaked courthouse steps. Not far from me was the town's claim to fame, a cement rendition of a pecan with its plaque declaring, "The World's Largest Pecan." As I stood there, I recalled another hot summer day when we drove down this same street, with the same pecan making the same silly claim, and similar people walking just as purposefully to their destinations—the bank, the insurance office, the bakery, the drugstore. That day we were bringing our firstborn baby home from the hospital. I remember being struck that people's ordinary lives were continuing when I was holding a miracle in my arms. My life, our lives, had just become so extraordinary! Today, twenty-three years later, I was party to the dissolving of the marriage that brought forth that precious child. The people who passed by—indifferent to my drama then as well as now—were engrossed in lives that looked normal; mine was not. I was about to go into the courthouse and forever change my identity, indeed, my life. And I did.

Suggestions:

- Have a plan for the rest of your divorce day. I first went to a garden party, then my son and I picked up the new car I had ordered, and afterwards we spent the late evening with some good friends in their back yard. (I may have overdone things a bit, but you get the message.)

- Remember that the divorce doesn't solve everything, but now, at least, you know that the indecision is over.

❧ Chapter Four ❧

Recovery

The last part of the divorce process is recovery. How can we recover? Do we ever fully recover? How long will it take? The pain surely does not subside the day of the divorce. That is indeed a watershed day legally, but it does not end our emotional roller coaster.

How long have you been in pain by the time the divorce actually takes place? How long has your struggle been going on? Of course, we need to expect that the aftermath from such sustained wounding takes a long time to heal. We need to heal in so many ways. Our lives are completely different now. In the first place, even the wars (within and without) we were having prior to the divorce gave us frequent contact with our now ex-spouse. That contact is gone. Also, these wars, including struggling with the decision to divorce and the business with our lawyers, gave our days and our thoughts substance, purpose, and direction. Suddenly, all that is over; now we are supposed to get on with our lives. But we are not ready for that. We feel empty and deflated. Poof! and whatever we had going on is gone. It's over.

Early Days

This is a dangerous time. Some of us sink into depression; the fight has gone out of us, and we can only see gloom ahead of us.

Twelve years after her divorce, Sue says her biggest regret about her divorce is the time she wasted being depressed about it. She literally crawled on the floor, whined, and felt sorry for herself for three years after the divorce. She finally pulled her life together, went back to graduate school, and is now happily teaching English in a community college. She has developed many friendships, enjoys concerts, plays, and dinner out with these friends, and has traveled extensively in Europe and Asia. Though she loved being married and never imagined herself a divorcee, she now loves her freedom and her life.

During this time others of us fill our lives and time with people, projects, work—whatever we can so that we don't have time to think.

Tom took on added responsibilities at work, volunteered for several committees, and filled his house with renters. He did not want to face the prospect of being alone with his thoughts and used his remarkable self-discipline and a full house to avoid thinking about what had happened in his life.

Other people make big decisions about our lives—we change jobs, we move to a new location, we quickly get ourselves into new relationships—all in an attempt to get on with life, to get past the pain, and maybe to prove to ourselves and others that we can take charge of our lives.

Elise, who didn't want to live in the same small community with her ex-husband and his girlfriend, moved across the country to the state where she had grown up and, once she had moved, she had to find a new job, a new house, and a new community of friends. Unfortunately, due to the stress of all she had been through, Elise developed serious health problems, which caused financial difficulties and limited her potential for full-time work. Now, six years later, she has adapted to her circumstances, and she is comfortably settled in her new community and her new life.

Too often we are in a hurry to move, whether this move is from one place to another, one job to another, or one relationship to another.

Kay moved quickly into a new relationship. She thought it would ease her pain and that it would be helpful to direct her attention to someone other than her ex-husband. Unfortunately, she still had to deal with her pain, but she had to do it privately because to talk about it openly would probably damage her new relationship. Other difficulties also arose. She had problems with trust, self-esteem, and the imbalance of power left over from her marriage and brought those issues with her. She didn't trust that her new partner would be faithful; part of that doubt stemmed from her former husband's infidelity and part of it came from her own left-over feelings of worthlessness. Because of her low self-esteem, she was still too anxious to please, too anxious about the other person's happiness. So, she again relinquished her share of power in the relationship, allowing the new relationship to be much like her last.

Perhaps we are in a hurry to move into another relationship because we are lonely and want to avoid that pain. Instead of rushing into another relationship, however, we should take the time we need (and it can take a long time) to move from lonely into an appreciation of being alone.

It's 12:45 A.M., and I am suddenly so pleased that I can stay up as late as I wish! I love being here alone! I can make noise whenever I want—I'm still not used to that. Soon the house will fill with the children and with company, and all that is good, too. But, for now, I'm enjoying my solitude and my freedom. I treasure these peaceful hours by myself in my snug, safe house.

✒

I'm alone in my silent house. I love the quiet. I wonder if I should read, grade papers, plan my weekend. I could exercise, eat, watch TV, draw, transfer names into my new address book, plan long term projects, or make lists! I could write letters. I love late nights, sunny days, morning coffee, and a newspaper. Now interruptions. I love those, too!

In addition to wanting to avoid loneliness after a divorce, we often seek the affirmation that a relationship seems to provide. (See? I am lovable!) But this is not the time to look for our affirmation from another love relationship. Another relationship will not solve the problems of the last one, and it is much better to bring a healed self to the next relationship than it is to bring a war-torn, damaged, uncertain self.

So, though we may desperately want to get on with our lives and get past our gnawing pain, we need to realize that the healing we need to do takes time, our time, regardless of how we try to avoid the issues. We need to regain our balance, our self-esteem, and find a new focus for our lives. We also need to learn to live with the scars that we now have.

Strategies that help the healing process:

- Set daily and long-term goals for yourself. Write them down and check them off when they are completed. Even small accomplishments help us feel good about our day.

- Take care of yourself. Exercise, eat well, rest, read, write in a journal, have a physical—you've been through a tough time.

- Stay in touch with your friends.

- Reach out, serve others (focus outside yourself).

- Plan a trip.

- Surround yourself with people who are sensitive and caring about your needs, and who laugh a lot. Don't let people dwell on the past if that is harmful to you. One night shortly after my divorce, some friends and I went out. One friend started telling me the latest news about my ex. I did not need that! I had terrible dreams that night and spiraled down into the depths the next day. If you aren't ready to talk or hear about your ex or your past, speak up! Remember, you will be the one to pay the price for the conversation.

THE AFTERMATH

What do we think of divorce later, after the deed is done? I have asked some friends this question and received a variety of responses.

Nan: "Divorce is not an option I would have chosen. Now, knowing the peace that comes with not trying to please someone who thoroughly disliked me, I would flee to it, poverty and all." She also said, "The problem with divorce is that it rips up our dreams for the future. It also tears apart the image we have of ourselves, who we thought we were."

Leah: "Honestly, I was never happy about how I was treated. I wanted him to be more loving to me. The fact is he must not have loved me for a long, long time and that was painful to finally realize and admit to myself. Now, after years and years, I am able to hope he will find someone he loves. I just don't want to hear about it."

Marlene: "Divorce was the most traumatic event in my life, but I am so glad I had the courage to leave my first marriage." She had nightmares for seven years after she remarried. In those dreams she was always forced to choose her first husband over her second. Finally, a friend told her that she was having those dreams because she could not acknowledge how horrible the first marriage had been. Following that comment, she never had another nightmare. She could always choose her second husband.

Jim: "I never imagined I would ever be divorced. I thought I'd married Mrs. Right." (His son quietly added, "You just didn't know her first name was Always.") Later Jim remarked that, though he had not wanted a divorce, now he mostly feels relieved and free, two feelings he hadn't even anticipated.

Chuck: "I felt (and feel) relieved . . . and guilty for feeling that way."

So, what do I believe about divorce? Divorce is never a perfect solution; it is never simply and purely right. It always involves breaking down a family and breaking a covenant. But sometimes it is the best choice and sometimes we are not really given a choice. When the abuse continues, the addictions remain, the affair is not ended, we need to consider that seeking a divorce is perhaps the most healthy response.

The Healing

How long does it take to heal? That is a question I have asked myself many times along the way. I've looked through my journal, trying to see if there was a straightforward progression from despair to healing. There was not. Some days I felt like I was healing, and the next day a memory would come to me that would send me right back to the pit. We must realize that we cannot let go of the past all at once; the letting go is also a process that does not occur in a straight line.

Four months after the divorce

Now I stand, divorced, with so many feelings. Sometimes the future looks hopeless and sad, but often it looks exciting and interesting. Day by day my feelings vary. I think that divorce was the right decision (most of the time).

Twenty-two months after the divorce

The day is gray. Snow again. I could use a blue sky and some jonquils and tulips today. I could wish for spring in my heart. How can some people sail through divorce?

Two-and-a-half years after the divorce

Ah, the flowering, the killing. The power of love and the devastation its abuse can wrought are beyond measure. Will I ever heal? It is two-and-a-half years since the divorce. Will twice as much time make any difference? Some difference? All the difference? I wonder.

Three years after the divorce

Oh, my broken-down life. It's a daily decision to embrace life, to go beyond the pain. I think divorce is something I'll never get over. So much is lost in addition to your mate: those many years of creating a family, a life within a community, shared hopes, dreams, the future, the present, the past. The connections that a couple weaves through years and years and years is all a torn, disfigured tapestry now—and I struggle daily to weave a new one, using all the scraps from the old that I can lay my hands on, and gathering a few new bits and pieces to create what I can.

✒

I think my tortured response to the divorce was largely because the purpose and goal of my life seemed utterly destroyed and denigrated. I lost my center and everything came tumbling down. Now I am at peace about my children, my family, and I am eager to find a new and meaningful purpose for my life. I have made so many big decisions lately—and I will continue to make them—and each one sets me farther down one path or another. New possibilities open and other possibilities are closed. Life is mysterious indeed. I love it.

❧

Now it is five years since the disintegration of our marriage began, three years since the divorce. Wow, how my life has changed. How I've changed. Now I can hardly imagine daily life with my ex anymore. Isn't that odd? Frankly, I think I am quite as happy as ever, at least most of the time.

Even when I wasn't happy, I discovered that my agony was less frequent, less intense, and of shorter duration the longer I was divorced.

Four years after the divorce

Memories of pain surge when I think back. Again I feel the pain, but not as fully and deeply, and it doesn't last. Time does help.

Five years after the divorce

Five years later. Would I want to go back if I could? Do I regret leaving? Should I have saved the marriage? Ah, life is mysterious. One can never know how other paths would have turned out, but I do know that I needed to flee the pain, the pain that nearly killed me. I needed a respite.

❧

Days fly by. I'm content much more of the time now. I think this life seems to be my life and not just a dream or a temporary invention. And I have discovered that here— in this new life—freedom, laughter, generosity, love, and serenity surround me.

When we see this new life of ours as mysterious, full of wonder and opportunity—regardless of circumstances—it is.

Six years after the divorce

As I look back, on the last two years of my marriage especially, I see what a destructive force was at work. Such mayhem! Why, I wonder. Oh, I just don't need to go through that door right now. It is enough to know that I am out of harm's way and the light of the world surrounds me, embraces me, and I am more whole than I was for too long. I feel like my life explodes with joys, opportunities, loved ones. I am so blessed.

I don't know that we ever fully get over our marriages; perhaps we shouldn't. I do think that we can move on and learn and grow so much from the divorce experience. If we don't, and we remain bitter or angry or dwelling on our loneliness, we cheat ourselves and those who love us. Instead, hopefully, we will embrace the new life we have and celebrate and cherish the gifts that are present in it for us and for those we love.

I love my aloneness, my freedom! It took a long time to get to this stage and state, but here I am. There was a time I didn't love life and never thought I would again, but now I love it deeply and reverently, as well as foolishly and joyfully. I just love life. What a gift. And for so long I didn't realize its worth!